SOME SHALL SOAR!

— Not Everyone is Called to be Average! —

By
Michael S. Pitts

THE WORD SHOPPE
CORNERSTONE CHRISTIAN CENTER
P.O. BOX 178380
TOLEDO, OH 43617

Unless otherwise indicated, all Scripture quotations are taken from the *King James Version* of the Bible.

Some Shall Soar!
ISBN 0-927936-14-3
Copyright © 1991 by Michael S. Pitts
Pitts Evangelistic Association
Box 178380
Toledo, OH 43617

Published by Vincom, Inc.
P. O. Box 702400
Tulsa, OK 74170
(918) 254-1276

Printed in the United States of America. All rights reserved under International Copyright Law. Contents and/or cover may not be reproduced in whole or in part in any form without the express written consent of the Publisher.

TABLE OF CONTENTS

Topic:

	Foreword	5
	Dedication	6
	Introduction	7
1	You Possess Seeds of Greatness	9
2	Dream Big!	13
3	Authority Begins on the Inside of You	15
4	Satan Doesn't Want Your Dream — He Wants Your Spirit!	17
5	Spiritual Bootcamp	19
6	Mount Up With Wings as an Eagle	21
7	Change Me, Lord!	25
8	You Can't Live Without "It"	27
9	Wisdom	31
10	Prosper Where You Are Planted	35
11	Withering Saints	37
12	Prospering Saints	39
13	Five Lessons From the Palm Tree	41
14	The Paralyzing Power of Pride	45
15	Jesus — Our Example in Resisting Satan	47
16	Another Side of Pride	51
17	Who is in Control?	55
18	Pride Prepares the Way for a Fall	57
19	Casting Off Pride	59

20	God Exalts the Humble	61
21	Two Kinds of Humility	63
22	Jesus Demonstrated Voluntary Humility	67
23	The Posture for Promotion	69
24	Maturing in God's Grace	75
25	Moving Steadily Forward	77
26	Jesus is Coming Again!	79
27	Refuse to be Offended	81
28	A Need For Integrity in Finances	85
29	Get the Star Dust Out of Your Eyes	89
30	Spiritual Warfare	91
31	Spiritual Authority	95
32	The Genesis Law	97
33	Submission to Authority	99
34	Edifying Communication	103
35	Judging Every Conversation	107
36	Energize Your Conversation With Positive Proverbs Power!	109
37	The Destructiveness of Repeating Negatives	111
38	Our Tent of Covering	113
39	Fitly Joined Together	115
40	Individual and Corporate Mentality	117
41	Accountability	119
42	Preserving Good Relationships	123
43	One Last Word!	127

Foreword

Michael Pitts is an up and coming leader in the Body of Christ. Even though he is a young man, he writes and preaches with the maturity of a well-seasoned veteran. In this book, he shares the wisdom and revelation God has given him for living a life of excellence.

The importance of this book cannot be overstated. At a time when the saints in the Body of Christ are longing and needing to stand up and exceed the norms of ordinary, mundane, day-to-day living, Michael Pitts has come forward to offer us a true Biblical foundation for realizing our dreams.

The Body of Christ has been waiting for such a time as this when God releases new leadership into the forefront. This dynamic book, SOME SHALL SOAR, will help every believer to go from "ordinary" to "extraordinary."

After reading this book, you will believe in your heart that God has really called everyone to soar!

Tim Storey

Dedication

This book is dedicated to the entire congregation of Cornerstone Christian Center. Your love and inspiration always encourage me to go for God's best every day. The joy of my life is being your pastor. I'm proud to call you *family!*

To our Children — Your faith gives me hope for the future. You are my treasure.

To our Youth — Thank you for your excitement to evangelize and stand for Jesus. You are my trophies of grace.

To our Seniors — Your zeal, wisdom and willingness to flow with God keep me going. You are my example.

To our Ministry Helpers — Only eternity will tell the story of how many lives have been touched because of your faithful service to the Lord's house. You are my hands and my heart.

To my Staff — Who run the everyday matters of the church so well I'm not sure if anyone would notice if I was gone. I think that is good.

To my Family — It's great to serve Jesus with those whom you love the most!

To the Holy Spirit — My partner every day!

Introduction

One of the most pressing needs in the world today is the need for *leaders*. Homes, businesses, governments and churches are all dwindling in the realms of average because of this void.

Nothing rises above the level of its leadership. Average messages by average pastors to average Christians have produced a generation of followers who are unable to lead the world out of the ditch many have fallen into.

It is my desire that you will receive your mandate from God to arise as a leader. I pray you will break free from the directionless crowd which lives in a religious stupor and that you will find purpose, productivity and power by living the Jesus life.

Michael Pitts

1
You Possess Seeds of Greatness

The hot August sun beat down upon the young lad as he walked slowly through the familiar grass of his daddy's Georgia farm. It was a day, not unlike others, filled with chores, cows, sweat, chickens and family. There wasn't much time for foolishness, but there was always time for contemplating, which is exactly what Junior had in mind as he finally reached his thinking spot.

His "thinking spot" was actually an ancient shade tree which stood alone on the peak of a large hill. Maybe it was the elevation of the land that caused his thoughts to escape and soar far above the familiar farmhouse now barely visible to the east. Or perhaps it was the feeling of history provided by the friendly old tree. Nevertheless, it was in this special spot that perspective was gained.

The shade of the tree and the rustling of its leaves provided a sanctuary of silence that neither busy hens nor rolling tractors could penetrate. Yet, looking down on the well kept acres of his family's farm, the lad couldn't help but notice how small it looked, especially when compared to all his eager eyes could see from his vantage point, far beyond the reach of everyday life.

It was in this place that grand plans were laid, dreams were dreamed and destinies were envisioned. All those big city governmental problems were put to rest and personal significance was evaluated.

Though his vocation and vision would change with each sacred trip to this isolated spot, one thing was sure.

Some Shall Soar!

He would never be able to stay in the farmland below, for he had stood on the mountain of limitless possibility.

Have you ever been to the mountain? Do you have a vision to be a person of greatness for God? Is there a dream of destiny in your heart? If so, wave good-bye to the land of limitations, and get ready to start on a journey in which you will turn your dreams into reality!

> **And God said, Let us make man in our image, after our likeness....**
>
> **Genesis 1:26**

This verse contains a startling truth you should know about. To be made in the image and likeness of God is the greatest seed for greatness. The divine stamp of God's nature is inseparably woven into your spirit when you are born again.

God is productive. He is always doing something positive. He is continually moving and on the go! Yet, so many of His people never reach their potential. Some are busy, yet unproductive. Others have no God-centered direction or plan of action. Still others are waiting for something to happen as they sit idly by, longing for the excitement and fulfillment that comes with spiritual growth.

You can be productive and accomplish great things as you seek the Lord to know His will for you and then pursue the fulfillment of it.

The Spirit of God spoke a great word for *you* through Jeremiah:

> 'For I know the plans I have for you,' declares the Lord, 'plans to prosper you and not to harm you, plans to give you hope and a future.'
>
> Jeremiah 29:11, NIV

How can you know God's intimate plans for you?

> **Call unto me, and I will answer thee, and show thee great and mighty things, which thou knowest not.**
>
> **Jeremiah 33:3**

You Possess Seeds of Greatness

A new day is unfolding before you because of your love for God and your desire to please Him.

2
Dream Big!

God likes dreamers. He is the Giver of new dreams and the Mender of broken ones.

I think it is in our dreaming that we move closer to the way God sees things, for in our thoughts, we are not limited by our faults, environment, resources or experiences. We simply skip everything in between from where we are now to where we want to be. In a brief moment, we see ourselves and our goals in their completed state.

The question then is not so much "Can you dream?" as much as it is whether or not you are motivated and empowered to act by virtue of that dream. If faith without works is dead, *then a dream without diligence is dead,* abiding alone.

Therefore, in seeing the final state of our dreams, we must never forget that we cannot dream away all of the growth, experience, diligence and maturity it is going to take to catch up with those grand dreams and see them manifest.

3
Authority Begins on the Inside of You

> ...he that ruleth his spirit [is greater] than he that taketh a city.
>
> Proverbs 16:32

Before anything will manifest in the natural, it must first start as a dream in the heart and mind of man, since it takes a man or woman to incubate and perpetuate a dream. Therefore, rather than give our first focus to the dream, I believe we should give it to the dreamer.

Man has seen great progress in the realization of his dreams. He has harnessed the natural resources of the earth to make his life easier, and he has propelled himself into studies far beyond the atmosphere of the earth. Yet, in all of his achievements, he has failed to harness himself! As fast as one problem is solved, he creates a hundred new ones. Sometimes he is his own worst enemy.

Many people, after receiving public applause for the greatness of their dreams, were later removed from the pinnacle of success because of personal failure.

On the agenda of first order of importance is to gain control over your own spirit. How many times have churches, families and countless other institutions been hurt because they got caught up in a person's gift or dream and neglected the development of character and maturity? God's Word provides the menu for character development and maturity.

4
Satan Doesn't Want Your Dream — He Wants Your Spirit!

We are in a real battle with Satan. His goal is not so much centered on stopping your dream as it is to destroy you, which, of course, will stop your dream.

Many people seem to be achieving great things, yet they are losing the greatest battle — the control of their own spirit. If you rule your spirit, you can yield it to God. If you rule your finances, they can be used for God. If you rule or exercise self-control in your emotions, they can be used for God. If you rule your own thoughts, God can use your mind. If you don't rule yourself, you can be sure that Satan will.

One of the greatest signs of ownership is the ability to give. You cannot give what you do not possess. If you are walking in self-discipline and you possess your own vessel, then you can give yourself to God.

> **That every one of you should know how to possess his vessel in sanctification and honour.**
>
> **1 Thessalonians 4:4**

Remember, you can't give to God for His use what you do not possess.

5
Spiritual Bootcamp

Babies and children aren't trained in the armed forces. Neither are those who are already wounded dressed for battle. People of potential are selected for training, regardless of race, religion or political persuasion.

Once enlisted, the men and women go through a training period called "bootcamp." This training process consists of a series of exercises to get men and women in shape, to build personal discipline, to shape their focus and to teach them to submit to authority. When they have completed this period of training, they are then moved into situations where they use the weapons and disciplines they have learned.

In the achieving of dreams, we often fail to realize that a battle for our own spirit is at stake. God doesn't give His armor, authority and power to children, babies or those who are wounded in their spirit. God has training laid out for you — bootcamp, if you will. Don't despise it. Accept the challenge to grow in self-control. Study the weapons of your warfare and the strategies of your enemy.

Paul said:

> For though we walk in the flesh, we do not war after the flesh:
>
> (For the weapons of our warfare are not carnal, but mighty through God to the pulling down of strong holds;)
>
> Casting down imaginations, and every high thing that exalteth itself against the knowledge of God, and bringing into captivity every thought to the obedience of Christ.
>
> 2 Corinthians 10:3-5

Learn to submit to authority, for one day you may find yourself in a position of authority.

Make a decision to be an excited, eager soldier. The bootcamp experience is a beginning step to the realization of your dreams.

God wants to guide you, lead you and teach you to dress in His armor. While fighting the good fight of faith for your dreams, you will rise above the real war, the battle for your soul. In Jesus Christ, eternal life is yours.

6
Mount Up With Wings as an Eagle

> But they that wait upon the Lord shall renew their strength; they shall mount up with wings as eagles; they shall run, and not be weary; and they shall walk, and not faint.
>
> Isaiah 40:31

The mother eagle's wings hesitated slightly in the updraft of warm air before folding perfectly as she came to rest on her nest. Some nest it was! Large and roomy, it was made up of pounds of brush, branches and countless other building materials she was able to scout out.

With patience that only a mother knows, she worked endless hours until she had woven, twisted and formed what once was simple vegetation into a fortress of safety. It rested majestically in the side of the rock-covered mountain aloft from most predators. The outside of this great resting place was a tangled web of thorns, thistles and sharp sticks.

Yet, it was on the inside of the nest that Momma really outdid herself. Hidden from view were the soft, warm pelts of rabbits, mink and other small mammals, which provided insulation from the environment and a cushion from the thorns which guaranteed their safety.

Time passed and what was once a quiet, empty nest became a home of activity. Hungry little mouths chirped, helplessly dependent upon Momma, so off she flew to gather a meal for her growing little eaglets.

All too soon the mother would look into her nest of love and no longer view tiny, helpless babies, but she would see strong wings and beaks emerge. She watched as they periodically climbed to the edge of the nest. Then, with their strong claws holding firm to the edge, they allowed the wind to blow through their expanded wings. While still protected by the home of the nest, they felt the sensation of the current for the first time.

If you asked the eaglets, all was well in the nest. Their mother fed them. They could experience the thrill of the current when they wanted and rest comfortably upon the warm fur which embraced them, but this became a problem area at a certain time in their growth. As long as she fed them and the nest was comfortable, they would always be dependent upon her and would never learn to fly.

One day, Mother came home and much to her youngins' surprise, she didn't bring home any dinner. They knew something was getting ready to change. With little more than a glance, Momma dived into the bottom of the nest with her chirping eaglets. Then she began pulling out all of the fur, throwing it over the edge of the nest. They had never seen such a sight. Yet, she persisted until all the soft lining of the nest was gone, exposing the sharp thorns beneath.

Now, there was some serious complaining going on! Did Mother stay around to hear it? No! She flew out of the nest and landed again on a cliff several feet above this curious sight. By now, each of the emerging eaglets had been stuck by an unfriendly thorn. The nest was no longer fun and comfortable, so they began to climb upwards toward its edge. What a sight to behold! The mouth of the large nest was lined with confused eaglets.

About the time they were ready to gather their senses together, Momma arrived on the scene again. She moved quickly toward one of her young ones perched on the edge, gave him a firm shove and out he went. Pandemonium and disbelief filled the nest. The same Mother who patiently built the nest and consistently fed the eaglets was now throwing them out! They thought, "Surely she knows we can't fly! Is she trying to kill us?"

In the meantime, a struggling eaglet plummets toward the earth. Momma jumps from the nest and dives like a bullet toward her first trainee! Just as the ground draws near, Mother swoops under her young one and catches him on the back of her wings. Can't you just hear that sigh of relief? His heart is glad, because Momma has come to her senses. Much to his surprise, she catches a warm draft of air and soars high above the nest and out over the dropoff of the cliff. With one sharp turn, she flaps her great wings and he spirals downward again.

One by one, this scene is repeated until the young birds realize they have wings to fly. Sooner or later, Momma won't have to bear them on her wings, but they will catch the current themselves and soar alone far above the nest of love. What a graphic illustration this is for those who would dare to dream of soaring as an eagle!

> **As an eagle stirreth up her nest, fluttereth over her young, spreadeth abroad her wings, taketh them, beareth them upon her wings:**
>
> **So the Lord alone did lead him....**
> **Deuteronomy 32:11-12**

Have you ever gone through a season of discomfort? Perhaps adversity poked at you or circumstances prodded you. If you are going to be great in God, there are times that God will stir your nest!

"Comfortable" is nice, and God certainly is a God of blessing, but is being blessed and feeling comfortable the same thing? I think not, for at the time of conversion, God immediately goes to work on you.

When I'm in a situation where my faith is being stretched and God is remolding some of my attitudes and character traits, my "flesh nature" is usually very uncomfortable. Yet, it is through this process where we learn to fly!

7
Change Me, Lord!

> **But we all, with open face beholding as in a glass the glory of the Lord, are changed into the same image from glory to glory, even as by the Spirit of the Lord.**
>
> **2 Corinthians 3:18**

What a wonderful promise we have from God that He will not leave us the way He found us! We will be transformed into His image.

Change can be disruptive and uncomfortable, yet it often sets the stage for the greatest of blessings.

God is so committed to see us mature in Him and be changed from glory to glory that He will stir our nest. If we're not ready to fly when He stirs the nest, He will swoop down and bear you up on His mighty wings. That's how much He loves you and me.

To achieve greatness in God often requires you to give up short-term comfort to gain long-term blessings.

Athletes have a saying, "No pain, no gain." Paul used phrases like, "...**endure hardness, as a good soldier of Jesus Christ**" (2 Timothy 2:3). "**I am crucified with Christ....**" (Galatians 2:20). "**Put on the whole armour....**" (Ephesians 6:11). These powerful passages, among others, indicate that it takes effort, discipline, determination and precision to soar with those of greatness in God's Kingdom.

This is the reason many people never walk in prosperity, power or peace. The blessings of God come as you work with the plan of God, which is for you to be changed so you can fly above the crowd of mediocre people.

If your desire for greatness is larger than your fear of failure or your love for the cushioned life, then mount up! God will provide the current if you will provide the wings!

8
You Can't Live Without "It"

I shall never forget the sight as he made his way down the steps of his corporate jet. Slightly stooped, yet full of life stood this great patriarch of faith. His hair was slightly thinner than the last time I met with him. A few lines, courtesy of the decades of ministry and travel, were now too noticeable to be denied.

As he steadied himself and walked up to me, I was struck again by his meek and peaceable spirit. Indeed, he was a man of power, authority and strength, yet so humble and gentle.

Many times while speaking with this "nameless" man of faith, I thought of the countless faces he had seen, the miracles he had witnessed, the obstacles he had overcome. I have long been an admirer of the longevity he personifies.

He began soaring years ago. With all of his powerful attributes, I saw one unmistakable quality. In my estimation, it is essential to achieve God's kind of success. It's something you must have! It's something that separates champs from chumps and eagles from turkeys. You can have "IT" if you make "IT" a priority. We will talk about "IT" in a moment, but first, let me tell you about another man who had "IT."

As a teenage preacher, I was in awe as I walked under his canvas cathedral. An old tent it may have been to some, but to the crowds of over 3,000 who filled it each night, it had become a symbol of the present-day power of God.

Some Shall Soar!

On one particular afternoon, I walked through the unoccupied tent filled with a sea of folding chairs. The fresh saw dust cushioned my steps as I made my way toward the front. Stretched out in front of the platform was a fifty foot by ten foot piece of red carpet. It was here that the real action took place.

Night after night, the suffering, sick, bound and oppressed lined up on this red carpet in hopes of receiving a miracle and receive they did! Many nights for hours at a time, this gifted man of God called out diseases and demons with the authority and boldness born from fellowshipping with God. The wear of the carpet testified to the multitudes of people who had jumped, clapped, danced or fallen as they came in contact with God's tangible power.

Miracles of every description and too countless to number were commonplace. Stories of visible manifestations of the glory of God and an anointing strong enough to stop a man's wrist watch added to the atmosphere in this setting. Anything was possible.

I was under the tent on this particular day, not so much for the miracles, but to see the man who had been God's instrument to perform them. It had been a long time since I had seen him, or more correctly, since he had seen me. My parents took me into his miracle services while I was still in my mother's womb. Once I was born, this man laid his hands on me and dedicated my life to God's service. Therefore, I returned to the Gospel tent to fulfill a sense of destiny and to acquaint myself with this man of faith.

As we met, I was taken off guard by his polite, yet somewhat formal demeanor. It wasn't exactly what you would expect from a "tent preacher." He had a charisma, a certain style or class, some would call it. Though up in years, his eyes were clear and his handshake was firm and steady. His face was as free of wrinkles as my heart was free of care. He looked remarkable.

We talked about the great crusades and the changing of the times. He lectured, instructed and warned me that day. Then, before we parted, he laid his hand on my head and said, "Father, let the anointing that rests upon me be upon him."

As I left that day, I didn't realize how many times in years to come I would witness evident characteristics of his ministry in mine.

I don't think the gifts are what makes the greatness of a person, though I am thankful for them. While speaking with this man and watching his life, I became aware that he too possessed the "IT" I am about to reveal.

Both of these older men had experienced some sense of longevity. It's not so much that young men don't possess it, as much as it is that the young don't become old without it. The "IT" I've referred to is *wisdom*.

9
Wisdom

> If any of you lack wisdom, let him ask of God, that giveth to all men liberally, and upbraideth not; and it shall be given him.
>
> James 1:5

The person who will do great exploits in God must walk in wisdom — not natural wisdom or even academic knowledge, but God's wisdom.

Wisdom is information guided by understanding. Noah Webster in his classic *1828 American Dictionary of the English Language* defines *wisdom* as:

1. The right use or exercise of knowledge.

2. Quickness of intellect; readiness of apprehension; dexterity in execution.

3. In Scripture theology, wisdom is true religion; godliness; piety; the knowledge and fear of God; and sincere and uniform obedience to His commands.

God is waiting and ready to release His wisdom in you. He is waiting for you to realize that your wisdom, precepts and plans are not adequate to fulfill His divine purpose. He is waiting on you to quit asking for His wisdom as a last resort. He wants His wisdom to dwell in you on a continual basis. Seek His wisdom first.

> But seek ye first the kingdom of God, and his righteousness; and all these things shall be added unto you.
>
> Matthew 6:33

Listen to what Solomon, the wisest man to ever live, wrote about wisdom in Ecclesiastes 9:16-18. He said:

1. *Wisdom is better than strength.*

Samson was a man of incredible super human strength. No matter how large the enemy may have been or how outnumbered he was, he always rose to the challenge and defeated all his foes by his strength. Yet, he was a man rendered powerless by one woman because he didn't walk in wisdom. Strength is good. Be strong, but above all, be wise.

2. *The words of wise men are heard in quiet.*

This tells me that much of our wisdom can come from other men. Wise men never feel the need to prove their position. Therefore, many times their words are drowned out by the loud, frequent cries of the fool.

> **Doth not wisdom cry? and understanding put forth her voice?**
>
> **Proverbs 8:1**

Wisdom is calling you today. Will you hear and be blessed?

3. *Wisdom is better than weapons of war.*

In Bible accounts, it is evident that God's people prevailed over their much more militarized enemies on many occasions. A weapon can help in battle if you have the knowledge of how to operate it. Yet, you must still understand *when* to use it and against whom to use it.

Wisdom is the primary key for success and longevity. Get it and keep it.

* It has many benefits (Proverbs 4:4-10).
* It gives happiness (Proverbs 3:13).
* It will keep you from evil (Proverbs 5:1-6).
* It is better than rubies (Proverbs 8:11).
* It is to be valued more than gold (Proverbs 16:16).
* It will give life (Ecclesiastes 7:12).
* It will make you strong (Ecclesiastes 7:19).

* It insures stability (Isaiah 33:6).

* It produces good fruit (James 3:17).

You need Proverbs power! The Bible has a lot to say about wise men and fools. Nowhere in the Bible is there a greater concentrated effort to impart wisdom than in the book of Proverbs.

The Proverbs power is simply this. Rise up every morning and read the chapter in Proverbs that corresponds with the day of the month. If it is the first day of the month, read Proverbs 1. If it is the second day, read Proverbs 2, etc. By doing this, you will not only read through the book of Proverbs every month, but you will also build a strong foundation for wisdom in your life.

You will find God's counsel on topics of relationships, money, child raising, associations, business matters, social justice, self-control and more. Your life will be long and successful if you interject Proverbs power into your life!

10
Prosper Where You Are Planted

Just as sowing precedes reaping and seedtime comes before harvest, so diligence precedes exploits and faithfulness precedes promotion.

> The righteous shall *flourish like the palm tree:* He shall grow like a cedar in Lebanon.
>
> *Those that be planted in the house of the Lord* shall flourish in the courts of our God.
>
> Psalm 92:12-13

It is God's desire for you to flourish and prosper, to excel, to reach your full potential and to soar. Anyone who knows about construction will tell you the higher you build, the deeper you dig the foundation.

Proportionate to your vision should be the strength of your foundation. Commensurate with your desire should be your dedication. Your commitment at home should match your calling abroad.

Many Christians are flighty. Their lives are governed by emotions and circumstances. When things are going well, they rejoice. When adversity arises, they are depressed. They give, pray, witness and attend church when they feel like it. Sometimes they disappear entirely from the picture.

One day they are singing, "I'm up on the mountain and I won't come down." The next day they are singing, "I'm down in the valley and I can't get out."

> ...For he that wavereth is like a wave of the sea driven with the wind and tossed.

> **For let not that man think he shall receive any thing of the Lord.**
>
> **James 1:6-7**

Paul's message in Ephesians 4:14 is very similar to James' message in these verses.

> **That we henceforth be no more children, tossed to and fro, and carried about by every wind of doctrine....**

Instability is a sign of immaturity. It brings a reproach upon the Lord and keeps Christians among the ranks of mediocrity. Stability is a sign of maturity. It brings the blessings of wisdom and longevity.

> **Therefore, my beloved brethren, be ye steadfast, unmoveable....**
>
> **1 Corinthians 15:58**

You should be planted, committed, steadfast and unmoveable in a local church. You cannot flourish in the courts of God until you are planted in His house!

11
Withering Saints

Withering saints do not prosper, they do not soar and they do not excel. They may hold a position, start a church or sing a song, but their instability will keep them from producing good, lasting fruit.

In Genesis 49, Jacob calls his sons to his side to pronounce his parting blessing over them. He begins with his oldest, Reuben. Look at this powerful statement:

> **Unstable as water, thou shalt not excel....**
> **Genesis 49:4**

Instability is found in the saints who run from church to church and from revival to revival. They are always looking for something new and spectacular. Those who are unstable pick their church like they choose a movie. They look in the paper to see what is happening (or showing). They are always on the move, following one fad after another, never staying anywhere long enough to be planted and taught how to mature and prosper.

12
Prospering Saints

> And he shall be like a tree planted by the rivers of water, that bringeth forth his fruit in his season; his leaf also shall not wither; and whatsoever he doeth shall prosper.
>
> **Psalm 1:3**

A true, full commitment to God will produce a deep devotion for His Body, the Church. As you allow God to plant you, stability will be produced in your spirit.

You will find yourself prospering, growing and maturing because of Your faithfulness to God in His house. Our generation needs to see examples of stability and longevity.

As you are faithful in allowing God to plant you, He will be faithful in watering you. *You will not be a withering saint! Whatever you do will prosper!*

13
Five Lessons From the Palm Tree

> The righteous shall flourish like the palm tree....
> **Psalm 92:12**

I want to share five lessons you can learn from the palm tree.

1. *The palm tree is not easily uprooted.*

As far as plant life is concerned, the palm tree is one of nature's toughest survivors. When all other vegetation withers, the palm tree continues to flourish. This is because its roots go deeper than other trees and plants. While an "average" plant's roots may only go feet or inches into the dry sand, the palm tree's roots extend hundreds of yards and sometimes a couple of miles in search of underground rivers.

The righteous are like the palm tree. If you allow yourself to be planted in God's house, your roots will grow deep. When tough times hit, other plants will dry up and wither away. Yet, you will continue to flourish because you have dug into the river of living water!

2. *You can cut the palm tree, but you can't kill it!*

Most trees have protective coating on the outside which we call "bark." If you cut a complete ring around a tree, removing the bark, minerals and nutrients will no longer pass to the rest of the tree. It will die.

Not so with the palm tree! Its strength is not in its outer shell. Its strength is in its inner core. You can cut it or carve circles around it, yet it will flourish because it has hidden strength.

The righteous are like the palm tree. The devil can cut you, but he can't kill you! People can cut you, but they can't kill you! Why? Because your strength is not in your outer shell — your body. Your strength lies deep within your spirit. You are tough! You are going to make it!

3. *The palm tree will bend, but it will not break.*

Tropical winds change very quickly. Sometimes they can exceed 70, 80 or even 100 miles an hour. With this type of wind, many trees snap and are blown away. Again, not so with the palm tree. As the winds increase, the palm tree bends, lessening pressure.

The stronger the wind, the further it bends. Sometimes it bends completely over until it looks as if the top will touch the ground. The palm tree bends, but it does not break!

When the powerful winds finally cease, the palm tree once again straightens to full height, actually made stronger in the place where it was bent.

The righteous are like the palm tree. You were made to outlast the storms and winds. They may bend you, but they can never break you. The adversities in life cannot destroy you, but they will only make you stronger!

4. *The fruit of the palm tree is preserved.*

Far above the reach of predators and out of sight of casual onlookers, the palm tree's fruit rests safely.

The righteous are like this palm tree. The enemy would like to steal your fruit and the rewards of your labor, but Jesus said:

> **Herein is my Father glorified, that ye bear much fruit....**
>
> **John 15:8**
>
> ...that ye should go and bring forth fruit, and that your fruit should remain....
>
> **John 15:16**

Five Lessons From the Palm Tree

God has placed the reward of your labor out of the reach of your adversary. You shall bring forth fruit, and it shall remain!

5. *Cold will kill the palm tree.*

With all of its strengths and attributes, there is one thing the palm tree cannot endure: the cold. It grows and flourishes only in warm climates.

The righteous are like the palm tree. God never made you to be in a cold climate. You must keep the fires of commitment burning. Keep oil in your lamp. Never become cold, critical and unconcerned. Pray without ceasing. Lift your hands up toward the Son and grow in the warmth of His love.

Find something to do, and be faithful and diligent in doing it. Do it with all of your might. Put your heart into it, and do it with excellence as unto the Lord. Dig deep! Fly high! But first prosper where God plants you!

14
The Paralyzing Power of Pride

> But He giveth more grace. Wherefore he saith, God resisteth the proud, but giveth grace unto the humble.
>
> Submit yourselves therefore to God. Resist the devil, and he will flee from you.
>
> James 4:6-7

Verse 7 says to *resist* the devil. It is not an option. If you resist Satan, he will absolutely flee from you. If the devil is always hanging around you, then you are not resisting him properly. If the devil is always after you, then you are not resisting properly.

Now, we used to have the mentality that said, "The devil only fights people who are fighting him, so if you are really spiritual, the devil will be after you all the time!"

I have found that Satan is somewhat of a bully. He will try to intimidate everyone. In other words, his attacks, like most intimidators, are not planned at the strong, but instead, he finds the weak — those he can bully — and maintains a defensive position.

Of course, it is also true that if you are aggressively going after the enemy, he will do all within his power to sway you. The good news is, *his power is limited.* All he can do is persuade, deceive and influence. He cannot make anything happen. Don't ascribe to Satan's power that which he does not have. He cannot read your mind. He cannot make you sick. He cannot take you to hell against your will. He will try to deceive, influence and persuade you to get into agreement with him. He knows something you need to know. *Satan can do nothing concerning you without your permission.*

You can break through into the victorious, overcoming life — a place where you refuse to be bullied and intimidated by Satan's schemes!

15
Jesus — Our Example in Resisting Satan

Jesus wasn't intimidated by Satan. Neither did He allow the devil to hang around Him all the time. The things Jesus did on this earth were done as an example for us of what we are to be and do.

Jesus was always victorious over the devil, because He knew how to resist Satan! When we resist like Jesus taught us to resist, victory will be ours.

In Matthew 4, Jesus was led by the Spirit into the wilderness to be tempted by the devil. Just as Jesus had to face Satan, in our walk toward maturity and greatness, we will have to face him, too.

> **And when he [Jesus] had fasted forty days and forty nights, he was afterward an hungred.**
> **Matthew 4:2**

Since the devil knows he cannot beat you in your area of strength, he looks for a weakness. In Jesus' case, going without food for forty days would produce some physical weakness. Therefore, this is where Satan begins his attack against Jesus.

> **And when the tempter came to him, he said, If thou be the Son of God, command these stones to be made bread.**
> **Matthew 4:3**

Without a moment's hesitation, Jesus began to resist the devil.

> **But he** [Jesus] **answered** [Satan] **and said,** *It is written....*
>
> Matthew 4:4

Jesus is teaching us how to resist. You resist the devil with the Word, *it is written*, and then quote the Scripture which applies to the area of temptation you are resisting.

In Verses 5-7, Satan continues his attack against Jesus. He takes Jesus to the pinnacle of the temple and tries to get Jesus to cast Himself down. Immediately, Jesus began resisting. He said, "**...It is written....**" (Matthew 4:7). Jesus resisted the devil with the Word of God.

Satan came after Jesus again in Verses 8-9, trying to get Jesus to worship him. Jesus stood against the devil's temptation with authority, because He knew if you resist the devil, he must flee.

Jesus said to the devil, "**...Get thee hence, Satan: for it is written, Thou shalt worship the Lord thy God, and him only shalt thou serve**" (Matthew 4:10).

Verse 11 reveals Satan's retreat. *"Then the devil leaveth him,* **and, behold, angels came and ministered unto him."**

The point I am trying to make is this: When Satan attacks, don't ponder or hesitate, but immediately resist him with the Word. Then command him to go. He has no choice because it is written that if you resist him, he *must* flee! Putting the Word on the devil will always cause him to retreat!

Resist does not mean you just sit back and wish the devil would go away. Your problems don't go away because you wish they would go away. *Resist* means "to actively work against the power that Satan tries to bring into your life."

With that in mind, let's look at James 4:6-7:

> **But he giveth more grace. Wherefore he saith, God resisteth the proud, but giveth grace unto the humble.**

Submit yourselves therefore to God. Resist the devil, and he will flee from you.

The word *resist* in both verses has the same connotation: actively working against.

The same spiritual law goes in operation with God when His people get into pride. When you get into pride, God resists you. That means, He *actively works against you.*

In this book, we have been talking about issues you must deal with in preparation to excel in God's Kingdom. God is not able to use those who think they are deserving of His anointing, for that is pride. Neither can God effectively use those who feel so inferior that they will not respond to God's invitation to soar. That, too, is pride.

16
Another Side of Pride

The reverse side of pride is saying you are nothing when God says *you are something!* It is amazing to me that we, as Christians, can sometimes be halted, because we don't understand God's principle of walking in humility. Most people's picture of humility is someone who is always talking bad about themselves. "Well, I am just a nobody. I am just an old sinner saved by grace."

If God has given you gifts and abilities, then you are supposed to speak and be in agreement with the will of God. If you are always running yourself down when God is trying to lift you up, then you are actually operating in pride, because pride, in its simplest form, is self-centeredness.

Let me show you how this kind of pride manifests itself. Let's look at Exodus 3 and use the call of Moses as a short case study.

Moses had been tending the flock of Jethro, his father-in-law, when God spoke to him through the burning bush. God told Moses that He had heard the cries of the children of Israel who were in bondage to Pharaoh. God's plan was to set them free, and He wanted to use Moses as His ambassador. God said to Moses:

> Come now therefore, and I will send thee unto Pharaoh, that thou mayest bring forth my people the children of Israel out of Egypt.
>
> Exodus 3:10

Listen to Moses' response:

Some Shall Soar!

> ...Who am I, that I should go unto Pharaoh, and that I should bring forth the children of Israel out of Egypt?
> Exodus 3:11

Moses responded in pride! "I" is the center letter of pride. Pride is being more concerned with how *you* feel or think, or about the situation than with what God has said about it.

God continued to unfold His plan to Moses, but Moses was still thinking about himself.

> And Moses answered and said, But, behold, they will not believe me, nor hearken unto my voice: for they will say, The Lord hath not appeared unto thee.
> Exodus 4:1

Moses' pride is showing a bit. He has himself at the center of this situation. God has gone through this same pattern with many of us. He tries to give us a mandate that requires obedience and faith, and all we can think about is, "What will people think? Will they believe us, or what will they say about us?"

God assured Moses that with signs following He would see to it that the people believed Moses, but Moses is still thinking about himself.

> And Moses said unto the Lord, O my Lord, I am not eloquent, neither heretofore, nor since thou hast spoken unto thy servant: but I am slow of speech, and of a slow tongue.
> Exodus 4:10

Pride always puts you and your will above God and His will. True humility, on the other hand, submits to and agrees with God's plan and will. Moses' focus was on himself. "Who am I? They will not believe me. I am slow of speech."

Humility agrees with God. If God says I am gifted, blessed and able to be a deliverer, then I agree.

The words of your mouth will reflect your belief in God's promises. You won't say, "I am slow of speech." Instead, you will say, "I am speaking for God!" You won't

Another Side of Pride

say, "Who am I?" but you will say, "I am the righteousness of God in Christ."

God has called people into the ministry who spend a great deal of time apologizing for what He has told them to do. "Well, now I hate to bring this message. If it was up to me, I would not do it. But if I don't do it, then God will get me." Apologizing for God's will is simply pride.

Why? Because you want people to look at *you* and like *you* and that is not him saying that, but the Lord must have made him say that. There was a man who got up to teach one day. He started making excuses because he couldn't teach. He got up and said, "I can't teach."

He was asked, "Why can't you teach?" "I am so nervous, and I don't want to do anything wrong." He went on and on with excuses.

He finally got to the place where he would teach, and people went to sleep. If you get up to teach and everyone falls asleep, then you aren't called to teach!

People thought this man was being humble. "He is so humble, he doesn't want to lift himself up." You must rise to a level of authority so people can receive from you. Some folks are walking around so low you can't even find them! I don't want someone who is falling apart to tell me how to live for God. I want someone who has found something in God.

"Oh, Brother Joe, he's so humble!" Do you know what the problem was with Brother Joe? He was more concerned about himself and how he was being perceived than he was about the people. Pride is being self-centered. Give it no place in your life.

17
Who is in Control?

We need to know what humility really is. Let me give you an example. I like to ride horses, though I don't get to do it very often. If I am going to ride a horse, I want one that's alive!

One year, my wife and I went to a ranch to go horseback riding. They brought out an old, fat, lazy-looking horse, the kind you have to drag out of the stable. They drug him out, but as soon as he came out, he wanted to go back in. I said, "Don't give me that old, fat, lazy-looking horse. I want one with some life in him. I want a horse who, when you say it's time to run, will run. I don't want a horse who is ready to be put out to pasture."

Horses have a great deal of strength. A person who likes horses will like one they call a "spirited" horse, one who has a little bit of life to him.

Then anyone who knows anything about horses knows it doesn't do any good to have a horse that is spirited if you can't control him. A spirited horse who can't be controlled isn't worth a dime.

A man who owns a great number of horses and has one he really likes because it is spirited and has a lot of life will have to get rid of it if the horse isn't teachable. He wants a horse to have energy and power, but if it won't come under its master's authority, it is good for nothing.

The horse has more raw strength than the one who is riding it, but he has to be subject to the rider. Even though the horse may have ability and great strength, he must learn to allow his strength to be brought under control and under subjection to the guiding force. Then it will be a productive horse.

This is a very good parallel, because God has made us "spirited" people. We are Spirit-filled people. Spirited people can be like wild stallions with no restraints. Some people want to be free from all authority and instruction and free to do whatever they want to do. You may be spirited, and God has given you power and authority, but unless you are under God's control and guidance, you are of no use to Him. He will find someone else to use.

Thank God for those who know how to allow that power to be directed by God to fulfill His plan in their lives.

18
Pride Prepares the Way for a Fall

> Pride goeth before destruction, and an haughty spirit before a fall.
>
> Proverbs 16:18

Pride was the sin of Lucifer. You can read about it in Isaiah 14:12-17 where we find pride statements or the five "I wills" of Satan:

1. I will ascend into the heaven.
2. I will exalt my throne above the stars of God.
3. I will sit upon the mount of the congregation.
4. I will ascend above the heights of the clouds.
5. I will be like the Most High.

God's response to pride is always the same. He resists or actively works against it.

> Yet thou [Lucifer] **shalt be brought down to hell, to the sides of the pit.**
>
> **Isaiah 14:15**

Satan's plan was to exalt himself, but God brought him down. Psalm 75:6-7 says:

> For promotion cometh neither from the east, nor from the west, nor from the south.
>
> But God is the judge: he putteth down one, and setteth up another.

19
Casting Off Pride

Some people walk around saying, "I am just a sinner saved by grace." Did you know that's not in the Word? You *used* to be a sinner. You *were* saved by grace. But if you are now walking around saying that you are "just a sinner saved by grace," you are wrong! People think it sounds humble, but it is pride.

False humility says, "You all pray for me. I can't really sing. Just listen to the words." If we are going to listen only to the words and you can't sing, then sit down, write the words down and we will read it in the bulletin.

A person is prideful who says, "I didn't want to be in the ministry, but the Lord just wouldn't let me get away from it. He kept after me until I finally said, 'Oh, yes, Lord.' " Who wants to hear what this person has to say?

Another area of false humility (or pride) is when someone says, "I just can't do anything." If God said you can do it, then bless God, *you can do it.* Genuine humility is saying that everything you have is a result of the gift of God. You glorify God by saying, "Thank You, God." It is God who makes you effective with other people.

You need to say, "Thank You, Lord, because You have given me the ability to touch someone on my job. Thank You, Lord, that You called me to be a leader, not just a follower." God is the Giver of good gifts to those who walk before Him with a humble spirit. He will lift that person up!

Some Shall Soar!

Better it is to be of an humble spirit with the lowly, than to divide the spoil with the proud.

Proverbs 16:19

Humble yourselves therefore under the mighty hand of God, that he may exalt you in due time.

1 Peter 5:6

20
God Exalts the Humble

Humility is ultimately placing God's will and His Word above your plans and your word.

Sometimes it is really hard to step off the throne of your life and allow God to speak something that is totally opposite of what you plan to do. It is easy to be in agreement with God when He tells you what you want to hear. God says, "Go and be blessed." You say, "Amen, God. I am in agreement with You." Then God says, "I want you to pray for someone who is despitefully using you." Suddenly, it is more difficult to be in agreement with God. So what should you do? Humble yourself.

God wants to exalt you. He wants His people to be exalted. God wants His people to be in places of authority. He wants His people to be the decision makers in the world. But He wants you to be exalted by humbling yourself before Him.

If a man lifts you up, then a man can bring you down. If people work to get you where you are, then people can work to bring you down. If God exalts you, then man can't bring you down. If God lifts you up, then the devil can't bring you down.

It is the Lord who gives direction to your life. You can say, "I am going to do this. I am going to do that. I am going to be here or there." You can get there, but the question is, *can you stay there?* If God puts you there, then you will stay where He puts you. If God exalts you, then you will always be in that position until He exalts you again. The fear of man won't affect you.

Many times, people get to the place where they are only to realize they owe people favors. That's not the blessing of God! You can move along politically in the structure of whatever you are doing and move to a certain level, but if you get to the top and you owe everyone favors, then you will not be effective for God because you have too much allegiance to everyone else.

If God lifts you up, then you can be His ambassador. You can speak when He wants you to speak. You can do what He wants you to do. You can do anything God says to do if He is the One who exalts you!

It is imperative that you find God's will for your life and then fulfill it God's way.

It is heartbreaking to watch people struggle and labor, trying to achieve something in their own effort that they will never accomplish. But if they would let God help them, they could achieve their goals for their family, business, church, etc. Many people leave God out. They want to do it their own way. They are too busy working hard to build their business. They don't have time for church.

When you think you can do something yourself, you are in pride. With all your laboring, you will not achieve great success. God resists the proud. But if you will put God first in all of your endeavors, He will give you grace. You will turn your hard work into smart work, which pays great dividends!

21
Two Kinds of Humility

We must learn what it means to walk in Biblical humility. There are two kinds of humility. One is *voluntary* humility, which means to humble yourself in the sight of God. The other is *involuntary* humility, which is when you become humble, but you weren't planning on it!

God has a way of insuring that we don't get too big for ourselves! The Bible says, *"A man's gift maketh room for him,* **and bringeth him before great men"** (Proverbs 18:16).

God wants your gift to be a blessing in your life. If God places a gift in your life, that gift will make room for you, but He can't make room for a big head!

Nebuchadnezzar found out about *involuntary humility.* Involuntary humility comes because of resisting God.

Nebuchadnezzar is credited with being the builder of Babylon, the first of four great empires. He was on top of the world. Everything he wanted he got. Every goal he set he achieved. But somewhere in the midst of all of his success, he forgot about God. He began to exalt himself. Therefore, God began to work against him.

Daniel 4 tells of a dream God gave the king which troubled him. In this dream, the king saw a tree of great height. It was strong, its leaves were fair and it bore much fruit. Then a Holy One from heaven came down to view the tree. The Holy One cried out, "Hew down the tree, cut its branches off, shake off its leaves and scatter its fruit."

Some Shall Soar!

Why does God work against pride? I believe the answer is found in Daniel 4:17.

> **This matter is by the decree of the watchers, and the demand by the word of the holy ones: to the intent that the living may know that the most High ruleth in the kingdom of men, and giveth it to whomsoever he will....**

The king summoned Daniel to interpret his dream. Daniel explained that the tree represented the king himself. He had become great, but God was about to cast him down.

> **That they shall drive thee [Nebuchadnezzar] from men, and thy dwelling shall be with the beasts of the field, and they shall make thee to eat grass as oxen, and they shall wet thee with the dew of heaven, and seven times [seven years] shall pass over thee, till thou know that the most High ruleth in the kingdom of men, and giveth it to whomsoever he will.**
> **Daniel 4:25**

In rage, the king spoke what was in his heart. He said:

> **...Is not this great Babylon, that *I have built for the house of the kingdom by the might of my power, and for the honour of my majesty?***
>
> **While the word was in the king's mouth, there fell a voice from heaven, saying, O king Nebuchadnezzar, to thee it is spoken;** *The kingdom is departed from thee.*
> **Daniel 4:30-31**

Within the same hour, God's Word was fulfilled. The man who once sat on the throne was out of his mind and running with the animals. His hair and nails grew long. People looked upon him with disdain. This state lasted for seven years.

God did not do it to him. He did it to himself. We are talking about *involuntary* humility. The good news is, Nebuchadnezzar did become humble.

> **And at the end of the days I Nebuchadnezzar lifted up mine eyes unto heaven, and mine understanding returned to me, and I blessed the most High, and I praised and honored him that liveth for ever, whose dominion is an**

Two Kinds of Humility

everlasting dominion, and his kingdom is from generation to generation.

Daniel 4:34

Success is a great thing when it is kept in perspective to the One who enables you to be successful! Don't forget the lesson Nebuchadnezzar learned. *God rules in the affairs of men, and He gives the kingdom to whomever He wills.* Write it down, memorize it and get it into your spirit. This is one of the greatest seeds for success you will ever learn.

When others try to hold you back, speak it out loud. When no one believes in your dreams, stand on them! When you have exhausted your resources only to find they weren't enough, trust in God! He is still the ultimate authority!

God alone holds the power to put one up and another down. Sometimes people think they are beyond God's correction because of their money, fame or position. Hear the words of King Nebuchadnezzar one more time.

Now I Nebuchadnezzar praise and extol and honour the King of heaven, all whose works are truth, and his ways judgment: and those that walk in pride he is able to abase.

Daniel 4:37

22
Jesus Demonstrated Voluntary Humility

> Let this mind be in you, which was also in Christ Jesus:
>
> Who, being in the form of God, thought it not robbery to be equal with God.
>
> Philippians 2:5-6

Now, watch His voluntary humility.

> But made himself of no reputation, and took upon him the form of a servant, and was made in the likeness of men:
>
> And being found in fashion as a man, he humbled himself, and became obedient unto death, even the death of the cross.
>
> Philippians 2:7-8

These powerful verses are very clear. Jesus was in a position equal with God. Yet, He chose to make Himself a servant. He brought with Him no great reputation. He walked in voluntary humility. Let this mind also be in you.

Remember once again the principle from 1 Peter 5:5. "**...God resisteth the proud, and** *giveth grace to the* **humble.**"

When you walk in voluntary humility, God goes to work on your behalf! The proof is in Philippians 2:9:

> "**Wherefore** [or because of Verses 5-8] *God also hath* **highly exalted him, and given him a name which is above every name.**"

Jesus understood how to get God's unlimited power to work for Him. Think what you could do if God worked for you in all of your endeavors. Jesus' voluntary humility and God's exalting Him were the focal points of Peter's great message subsequent to the first outpouring of the Holy Spirit in Acts 2.

Peter drove home a powerful point. He wanted the men of Israel to understand that Jesus was not the victim of an angry mob, nor was He helpless to defend Himself against the political and religious evils. A sacrifice is only a sacrifice if it is *given* — not when it is taken! Peter said:

> **Him, being delivered by the determinate counsel and foreknowledge of God....**
>
> **Acts 2:23**

Jesus said of Himself:

> **No man taketh it** [my life] **from me, but I lay it down myself. I have power to lay it down, and I have power to take it again. This commandment have I received of my Father.**
>
> **John 10:18**

Now, let's look at Acts 2:32: **"This Jesus hath** *God* **raised up...."** Jesus was able to lay His life down without fear of failure. He knew God would bring Him out of the grave.

* He knew if He humbled Himself, God would exalt Him.

* He knew if He would lay down His life, God would give Him life.

* He knew if He laid down His reputation [His name], God would give Him a name above all names.

Father, let this mind be in us!

23
The Posture For Promotion

Today is the day to break the crippling power of self-promotion and self-aggrandizement. Find the posture for promotion. Give God an inroad into your affairs, and He will make room for you.

> If my people, which are called by my name, shall humble themselves, and pray, and seek my face, and turn from their wicked ways; then will I hear from heaven, and will forgive their sin, and will heal their land.
>
> 2 Chronicles 7:14

The posture for promotion is *prayer*. Humble yourself today. Call on God, and in due season, He will lift *you* up.

God says that no weapon that is formed against you will prosper (Isaiah 54:17). In ancient days when the people went out to war, they spent time in making their weapons. They put them into the heat. Then they would beat on them and form specific weapons geared toward coming against the weakness of their enemies.

The enemy knows your weakness. He doesn't suddenly come on you. He spends time cultivating that weakness in your life. He spends time trying to get a door open for that weakness to manifest. The entire time, he is forming a weapon geared to attack your weakness. But God says, "Let him form his weapon, because no weapon that is formed against you will prosper."

When the weapons are being formed against you, sometimes you want to say, "I have a right to be angry. I have a right to come against you." God says, "Why don't you humble yourself? Let Me take care of it."

Some Shall Soar!

All that is being formed against you has no power over you. Humbling yourself is a key to disarming the enemy. When I first began in the ministry, I figured if God called me to preach, then that is what He called me to do, and I would go anywhere to preach. A whole lot of people that I knew in the ministry started preaching when I did. They would go to some of the great places to preach, while I was preaching in garages.

On my part, I made a decision. It was voluntary humility. "I am going to do whatever God tells me to do." I remember a time when I was real frustrated and I was thinking, "Lord, am I doing the right thing?" One of the worst things you can do is look at someone else's life and compare it with your situation.

Have you ever seen people who are just nasty old sorry sinners, and they seem to be doing better than you are? This is a problem David faced. He said:

> Lord, how are they increased that trouble me! many are they that rise up against me.
>
> Many there be which say of my soul, there is no help for him in God....
>
> Psalm 3:1-2

The Lord taught David a lesson. The Lord basically said, "Let me take care of the unrighteous, and I will take care of you."

I began to do whatever God wanted me to do, and I found out that it was being a servant and being faithful in whatever He asked me to do that was preparing me for what He wanted me to do later.

When we humble ourselves, God can teach us something. One of the greatest hindrances in any area of life is to become unteachable. If you are unteachable, man can't teach you anything, God can't teach you anything, the pastor can't teach you anything, and your employers can't teach you anything because of pride.

The Posture for Promotion

When you are humble, you will say, "I am going to learn something. I have purposed in my heart that every place I go I am going to learn something." In many places, I learn what not to do. Then, in other places, I learn what to do. I begin to minister and make myself a servant. My attitude is, "God, I am going to be a servant. Whatever You want me to do, I'll do."

When we were doing tent meetings, Pastor Robert would stay about ten days under a tent to watch it. Have you ever watched a tent? You actually do nothing but watch it. We were in a city where if you left the tent by itself, they would come and burn it down or tear it down, so someone had to stay for ten days and live in the back of the bus. We called him Robinson Crusoe.

Someone had to watch the tent. I know a lot of people who could have done it, but they were too proud to do it. They said, "Bless God, I am not staying in that bus."

Remember, God resists the proud. No one would get saved if the tent wasn't on the ground. No one would get healed if the tent went up in flames. Someone had to watch it.

There are a lot of things where God gives glory and grace to people who we never think about. We may not even see it. God always uses people who are usable. He can use us if we will become willing and obedient to do the smallest things and become what He wants us to be, and if we will put our will exactly in line with His will.

If you will humble yourself unto God, He will exalt you in due season, and He will bring you to a place where your gift will make room for you.

I would go to Campmeeting where they had all these great men of God as speakers. I would think, "Boy, they are somebody!" I would pray, "God, I want to do what You want me to do."

Some Shall Soar!

I was called and asked, "Would you mind preaching at a certain daytime service?" I said, "No, I don't mind. I will preach whenever you want me to preach." Now, the day services weren't as big as the night services. Some of the preachers asked, "Do you feel bad because you are doing the day services?" I said, "No. The day services are just as anointed as the night services. We are having a great time."

I purposed in my heart to be a servant, even to the "big" Campmeeting speakers. You see, *if you realize who you are in God, it isn't hard to serve someone else.* If you can't serve someone else, you are lifted up in pride.

The last three years, I have preached at the same Campmeeting with Brother Sumrall, and I preached in an evening service. He preached one night, and I preached one night. That's pretty good, isn't it?

Do you know why God does things like that? I have seen people fall by the wayside who tried to exalt themselves. I have seen churches do the same thing. I can't come to your city and say, "I just don't know what we are going to do" when I know what God told me to do. That would be pride.

I believe God has called Cornerstone to be the largest Full Gospel supernatural church in our area. That's not pride. I am just agreeing with God. But God didn't call us to walk around with our spiritual chest out saying, "Look at us." If we get over into pride, God will resist us.

I don't care how good you can sing, preach or dance. You can't accomplish anything if God resists you. But if you will humble yourself and say, "God, I want to do whatever You want me to do," you will be a servant and maintain a servant's heart. Then people who have needs will seek you out. Praying for the sick is ministering and being a servant to those people. That is what preferring your brother is all about.

The Posture for Promotion

The disciples came to Jesus and asked, "Of all the people you have, who is the greatest?" The Lord said that whoever would be servant of all was the greatest of all. Whoever will abase himself and say, "I will do whatever God wants me to do" is greatest of all.

Remember when Jesus washed the disciples' feet? That was a great act of humility and servanthood. Peter, filled with pride, said, "**...Thou shalt never wash my feet....**" (John 13:8). Jesus said, "**...If I wash thee not, thou hast no part with me**" (Verse 8).

We've got to tear down the walls of pride in our lives. Pride will keep you from serving God, and it will also keep you from God. It keeps a person who knows his life is falling apart, who knows hell is a reality and who knows God is a reality, from giving in to God.

To be what God wants us to be, pride has no place in our lives. God will actively work against the proud, but He will give grace to the humble. God will clothe the person in His glory who is wrapped in humility. Then when the proper time comes, God springs it forth, everyone sees it and wonders how it happened. God says, "I give grace to the humble." He says, **"If my people, which are called by my name, shall humble themselves..."** (2 Chronicles 7:14).

Today is a good day to cry out to God in humility. Humble yourself and cry out to God on behalf of the people in your city. Cry out for those who don't have any direction in their life and for those who don't know God.

There are people who are in bed instead of in church whom God has destined and marked to serve Him. There are loved ones in your home who ought to be in church, but they are bound by something. Why aren't they set free?

God is looking for someone who will humble himself and be more concerned over the salvation of men than over "my ministry" or "my blessing."

Some Shall Soar!

Rise up and say, "God, I am going to pray for someone today. I am going to minister to someone today." Whatever you give toward someone else, God will return to you. Satan has no power to destroy people if we won't let him. He doesn't have the power to destroy my life unless I stop resisting him, but if I resist him, he has no choice but to flee.

24

Maturing in God's Grace

But unto every one of us is given grace according to the measure of the gift of Christ.

Wherefore he saith, When he ascended upon high, he led captivity captive, and gave gifts unto men.

(Now that he ascended, what is it but that he also descended first into the lower parts of the earth?

He that descended is the same also that ascended up far above all heavens, that he might fill all things.)

And he gave some, apostles; and some, prophets; and some, evangelists; and some, pastors and teachers;

For the perfecting of the saints, for the work of the ministry, for the edifying of the body of Christ:

Till we all come in the unity of the faith, and of the knowledge of the Son of God, unto a perfect man, unto the measure of the stature of the fulness of Christ:

That we henceforth be no more children, tossed to and fro, and carried about with every wind of doctrine, by the sleight of men, and cunning craftiness, whereby they lie in wait to deceive;

But speaking the truth in love, may grow up into him in all things, which is the head, even Christ:

From whom the whole body fitly joined together and compacted by that which every joint supplieth, according to the effectual working in the measure of every part, maketh increase of the body unto the edifying of itself in love.

Ephesians 4:7-16

As Christians, we are to come into the unity of the faith and to the knowledge of the Son of God unto a perfect man. The word *perfect* means "mature."

God wants His people to come to the place where they will edify and strengthen one another. There are things in the Word of God that God has reserved for those who have determined to grow in grace and in knowledge of the Lord Jesus Christ. Everyone will not succeed, even though it is God's plan for everyone to succeed. Only those who make a real commitment to personal growth in Christ will achieve the success in maturity which God has planned.

The Bible says that even Jesus Christ Himself "**...increased in wisdom and stature, and in favour with God and man**" (Luke 2:52). We also need to increase in wisdom and stature and in favor with God and man.

It's time to break out of the ranks of mediocrity. God wants you to develop your mind, spirit and body so they won't become lazy, slow and unresponsive.

I pray that God, through the power of the Holy Spirit, will birth in you a hunger for a more personal, intimate relationship with Him.

25
Moving Steadily Forward

We are living in a day when many voices can be heard, many which contain a thread of truth. Yet, those who would soar must learn how to stand on the foundational truths of the Bible and not allow themselves to be pulled from side to side.

God's plan is for you to go forward, straight ahead — not back and forth. Sometimes "moves" hit the Christian community with such impact that if one is not careful and discerning, they will be blown off course. God's truth will continue, while man's doctrine will dissipate. God's truth builds character, while man's doctrine builds on gifts and/or emotions.

> THE EMPHASIS OF ONE TRUTH
> TO THE EXCLUSION OF ALL OTHER TRUTH
> CREATES AN UNTRUTH.

In many cases, God can't give us what we are asking for, because we're not ready for what we're asking for. Noah could have said, "God, send the rain that You told me You were going to send," but God wasn't going to send the rain until Noah prepared the ark so He could preserve the lives of Noah and his family.

Sometimes we pray, "God, let Your glory come in its fullness. Then we begin to realize that if the glory of God came in its fullness, the Body of Christ wouldn't know how to handle it.

Many times, the Kingdom of God, as a whole, has been in the hands of those who know the least about it. When

God desires to do something, those who aren't mature in God go off in one direction, tossed to and fro, and take what God meant to be a truth, and they carry it completely out of balance. Others who aren't grounded in the Word are tossed to and fro. God doesn't want us to go to and fro. He wants us to go forward.

There is always a balance in the things of God. Our zeal can lead us from one extreme or another. As I have viewed the Body of Christ, most of the time we aren't consistently down the middle where God wants us to be. In other words, instead of being consistently in the middle of the road, the Body slips into one ditch and then the other for a while, getting off course and into error.

If you have been saved more than a year, you can probably think of times in your life when you were out of balance. I have been in that boat. When I was first saved, I had a lot of zeal and little knowledge. I wanted to do everything for God, but I didn't know how.

It's truly amazing that our relatives ever get saved, because of the self-righteous attitude most of us have come across with when we were first saved. You can't talk to them for 30 seconds without saying how hot hell is, why they are going there and why you aren't. We also have a way of communicating even when we don't say it.

There are many areas of imbalance in the Body of Christ, so many, in fact, that I can't cover them all. Yet, the principles involved from the examples I do share can be applied to many areas. The examples I share are not meant to criticize or condemn. Yet, a honest look at our tendency for extremism is a healthy remedy for our future.

26
Jesus is Coming Again!

In this hour, the daily newspapers are beginning to read like they have been extracted from Matthew 24. We sit in our homes and eat our dinners affected little or not at all as we view the ruins of another earthquake or see yet one more bloated-bellied baby dying of starvation.

Frustration mounts as we look upon an increasingly secularized society. Faith rises as we labor for the great harvest. In the midst of it, we have a blessed hope - the appearance of our Lord and Savior, Jesus Christ!

It is in a faith-charged atmosphere that prophecies and predictions about the Lord's return seem to flourish. Predicting His return is not our primary concern, for surely He is coming. But it is when self-appointed prophets begin to announce to the world *when* He is coming that trouble and confusion are stirred.

Everyone should know by now that no one knows exactly when the Lord will return. Yet, every now and then a fresh wave of end-time prophecies roll in, smashing many a ship into the rocks of extremism.

Some people have built bomb shelters and filled them with dehydrated foods to preserve themselves during the reign of the antichrist.

In every generation, someone has matched letters with the numbers 666, identifying who they believe the antichrist will be.

Through twisting Scriptures in Daniel and Revelation and adding some mathematical gymnastics, some have come up with the year, month and even the day of Jesus' appearing.

Those who believe they know the day of the Lord's return grow more extreme as the date approaches. The reports are numerous of people quitting jobs, selling all of their possessions and spending all of their savings only to be sadly disappointed.

Jesus said, in reference to the day of His return:

> But pray ye that your flight be not in the winter, neither on the Sabbath day.
>
> Matthew 24:20

Their "flight" as Jesus called it, is to precede His appearing. If there is a set day on God's calendar for Jesus' return, why would He instruct them to pray about the time frame which would precede it? If God has already set a date, prayer will not change it.

Jesus said:

> But of that day and hour knoweth no man, no, not the angels in heaven, but my Father only.
>
> Matthew 24:36

If the Father hasn't revealed to Jesus when the time of His return will be, I find it highly improbable that He has revealed it to anyone else. If God was going to reveal it, it would not be so a bunch of folks could sell their homes, quit their jobs and have one last fling.

Jesus is coming soon. That's a fact. But it is His job to find out when. It is our job to work until that day comes.

> Therefore, my beloved brethren, be ye stedfast, unmoveable, always abounding in the work of the Lord....
>
> 1 Corinthians 15:58

27
Refuse to be Offended

In the break room, normal conversations vary from children to strong coffee. Today, the conversation has turned to the Church. Co-workers become quiet as Brother Christian mentions taking the family to church on Sunday. Here and there, sporadic questions are asked as he talks. "What is the name of your church? Who is the pastor? What time did you say it started?"

Marked behind the co-worker's simple questions are cries for help. People's lives are hurting. Their families are hurting. Inside, a growing sense of hopelessness drives them into the clutches of a spirit of fear, so they ask their questions hoping Brother Christian will share some living water with some thirsty friends.

To their surprise, no invitation is given and no prayers are offered. His voice is lifeless. His face is tense and sneering. His words are cynical and cutting. Brother Christian has no time for them today. He is too busy licking his wounds. He has been offended.

As the workers returned to their separate tasks, not one of them could remember why Brother Christian was offended. Just that he was, so they work on, a little slower than before. They had been poisoned by the man's offense.

It didn't matter to the sinners whether the new sanctuary addition was a rectangle or a square. They didn't know the choir's song was inappropriate. As a matter of fact, they had no opinions concerning the color of the carpet or the volume of the music. They didn't care that the pastor had a new car.

So Brother Christian, once a vibrant, energetic witness, is now reduced to one of the religious regiment. The sinners struggle on, still hurting, hopeless and thirsty.

God's people spend too much time being offended. Neither you, nor one who plans to soar, can afford to be weighted down. You must learn to shake off every offense as quickly as it comes.

There isn't a person living who hasn't been faced with an opportunity to be offended. It is what you do with your opportunity that makes the difference. Every time someone wrongs you, you can either become bitter or better. The choice is yours.

Some people live in a realm of offense. Someone, some church, or something hurt them, and they have never let go of it. Therefore, they are trapped and chained to that offense because of unforgiveness. They judge everyone in light of their offense. They make decisions based upon their offense, and their feelings are controlled by their offense.

An offense can hold you only if you walk in unforgiveness. Most of the time, if someone is offended, they believe whoever offended them should change. Yet, the truth is, the one who is always being offended needs to grow up and forgive!

Jesus stated in the explanation of the parable of the sower that a person can become offended if he has no root in himself (Matthew 13:21).

My wife and I have built our lives and ministry on Psalm 119:165.

> **Great peace have they which love thy law: nothing shall offend them.**

Because I want to do great things for God, I don't have time to be offended. You might think that sounds easier to say than to do. I agree, but it is the only way to stay free. You must forgive and shake off offenses.

Has someone in the church hurt you? Has a man or a woman walked out of your life? Have you been the victim of prejudice? Did someone involve you in a business venture only to sell you down the river? Were you molested as a child?

Satan comes to put offenses into your heart in so many different ways, yet God wants you to be free. Completely free!!!

You can break the power of offense by:

Remembering — Just because you have the right to be offended doesn't make it right for you to be offended! It is better to be wrong and walk in love than it is to be right and be offended!

Repenting — Ask God to forgive you for allowing the seed of offense to grow in your heart. If you have spoken evil of those who offended you, make a decision to change.

Releasing — God can forgive you only as you forgive others. Release them from your judgment, and God will release you from His. Take it out of your heart, give it to the Lord and don't take it back from Him.

Rejoicing — It is easy to be happy if you are free. Start a new day knowing for the rest of your life you really can be free *every day.*

28
A Need For Integrity in Finances

God is a good businessman. He knows how to get things done, and He knows how to pay for His projects!

The terms *soaring* and *flying* bring pictures of freedom, while terms like *debt* and *indentured servant* speak of bondage.

GOD WANTS YOU FREE
IN YOUR BODY
IN YOUR SPIRIT
IN YOUR FINANCES.

Sometimes Christians become so wrapped up in the development of their gifts and abilities that they neglect to take proper care of their business.

Many a gifted person has been limited in the expression of his gift by poor business dealings. It doesn't matter whether you are in the five-fold ministry, in a leadership position in your local church, or a lay person who just wants to be the best witness you can be. Finances and how you handle them will play a major role in your effectiveness for Christ.

There is only one thing worse than a Christian who won't pay his bills and that's a minister who won't pay his bills!

There are many reasons why people are slothful in business, but let me share the three most common reasons with you. People are slothful in business because:

1. They don't feel it is that important or spiritual.

2. They believe if God wants them to succeed, then they will.

3. They are moving ahead of God's will. In other words, they want everything *now.*

Proverbs 22:29 should give you greater understanding of the importance of diligence and integrity in business.

Seest thou a man diligent in his business? He shall stand before kings; he shall not stand before mean men.

Meditate on this Scripture until you get it into your spirit. God is concerned about the way you handle your finances, and He wants to be your business partner. You will do much better with God on your side, like Abraham, Joseph, David, Solomon, the boy with the loaves and fishes and the widow woman of Zarephath.

When you invite God to get involved in your finances, He will bring you into a place of authority and blessing. How do you get God involved? By applying His Word to your business.

Now let's get back to the three misconceptions about the handling of your finances.

1. *People don't feel business is important or spiritual.*

God places a high priority on how you handle your finances. If you treat the natural resources God gives you lightly, you will probably treat spiritual things lightly.

Some of the greatest preachers in the world are unsuccessful because they treat business lightly. If your business isn't in order, you are giving place for the devil to take what God has given you. That is why God watches to see what kind of a steward you are. He wants to put you in authority over many things, but He doesn't want to give you something only to see Satan steal it because you weren't diligent about God's gifts.

Proverbs 12:24 says:

The hand of the diligent shall bear rule: but the slothful shall be under tribute.

2. *Some people believe, "If God wants me to succeed, I will."*

God does not get everything He wants. If He did, everyone would be born again, healed and blessed.

God tells us what His will is in His Word. Then we must diligently apply Scripture to achieve His will in our lives.

God placed a choice before us in Deuteronomy 30:19:

I call heaven and earth to record this day against you, that I have set before you life and death, blessing and cursing: therefore choose life, that thou and thy seed may live.

The decision to walk in God's provision is yours. Whatever state you find yourself in right now is a result of the choices you have made in the past — some good, some bad.

If I am where I am today because of what I did yesterday, then I can change where I will be tomorrow based upon what I do today!

3. *They are moving ahead of God's will. They want everything now.*

You cannot do everything at one time. Some things are good ideas, but that doesn't mean they are in God's will for you.

I know pastors who get involved in every meeting that comes to town. They support every community project that is presented.

Some traveling ministries believe if they could only get on television, it would really build their ministry. Now, certainly God has spoken to many ministries to do just that. Yet, if a person walks in presumption and creates large TV bills and leaves God to pay for them, they are wrong.

There is a time for every vision to come to pass. If God is in it, the blessing will be there. If you are doing something that isn't being blessed, ask yourself a few questions:

1. Is it set in proper order?

2. Did God tell me to do this?

3. Is this *when* God told me to do it?

4. Is this *how* God told me to do this?

God put it in my spirit to encourage His people to put themselves in a strong financial position. When you own something, no one can take it from you. When you are in ownership, you can act like God acts.

Start today. Don't delay. Develop a plan for financial freedom and walk in it!

29
Get the Star Dust Out of Your Eyes

My mind has sometimes drifted to the day when the Lord will hand out rewards for service on earth. Every saint will be there. Some will be well known for their achievements. The faces of some will be easily recognizable. Others will be drowned in a sea of anonymity. Grant me the poetic license to expound.

The buzzing of happy conversation will be stilled as great recognition is paid to a faithful soldier of the cross. Crowns, robes, gold and even a new name will be given to him.

"Who is it?" people will ask. All will answer, "I don't know." Maybe it was that guy you always thought was a little different. You know, the one who faithfully drove the church bus through rain, sleet and snow for many years.

Maybe it was the senior citizen who sat alone in the church every week, the one you never could find the time to talk to. She never forgot you, though. She spent many years in intercession.

Maybe it was that young preacher who spoke only one night at your church. He was the fellow you had never seen on TV, and he had never written a book, so you stayed home to catch up on some things.

Maybe it was a faithful nursery or Sunday School teacher who never heard the words "thank you."

Maybe it was a teenager who had been a bold witness against the press of the crowd.

Maybe it was the woman who never lost her joy while trying to keep her three children in church and her home together, all the time living in poverty with an alcoholic husband.

Then again, maybe the name that was called was yours!

Don't allow your sight to become clouded with star dust. Please understand what I am saying. I am not against those who have risen to such a level that they are household names. Most people would not have made it to such a place of prominence, except they were faithful to their calling. Thank God for them.

Yet, it is important to understand that God has not called everyone to be on TV or to be in the ministry. However, God has called everyone to *excellence, faithfulness* and *servitude*.

Do whatever you are asked to do cheerfully and skillfully, knowing God's rewards are ahead, some in this life, some in heaven.

30
Spiritual Warfare

> For we wrestle not against flesh and blood, but against principalities, against powers, against the rulers of the darkness of this world, against spiritual wickedness in high places.
>
> Ephesians 6:12

Much is being said today about spiritual warfare. It is encouraging to see Christians who refuse to be dominated by Satan's power. We are learning to fight the good fight of faith.

There are three primary things you need to know about spiritual warfare.

1. *Our conflict is not with flesh and blood.* Today, more than ever, men and women are being bombarded by spiritual forces that try to motivate, influence and ultimately control them. It is very important that you are able to distinguish between the cause and the effect. What you see and know with your natural senses is the manifestation or the effect. Yet, behind the scene, demonic forces are at work.

Don't be moved by what you see. Be moved only by what you know in the Word. Then deal directly with the cause.

2. *Anything you won't fight to get, you won't fight to keep!*

It seems to be human nature to place little value on things we haven't had to work for. Easy come, easy go! If what you hope to achieve is not worth fighting for, it is not worth achieving. There is a price to be paid for every dream that is realized.

In God's Kingdom, the only people who fail are those who quit fighting.

3. *If you will fight, you will win!*

God has postured you for victory. It is not His plan that you ever experience failure.

Even the unrenewed man has some power over the devil. That's right. Every person has a human will. If you "will" to do something, you can do it. You are a free moral agent, which means God will not violate your will. He will not make you serve Him. He will not make you witness, go to Africa or marry a particular person. You must voluntarily say, as Jesus did, "Not my will, but Thy will be done, Lord."

God needs your permission to effectively guide your life. The same is true of Satan. He cannot superimpose his will upon you without your consent.

Some people have been bound by drugs, alcohol, sexual perversion, etc. The day comes when they make a declarative statement born out of their human will. They say, "*I will* not drink again. *I will* not fall into another improper relationship. *I will* not smoke."

You probably know someone like that. They are not born again. They just reformed some of their habits by an act of their own will. If the unrenewed human will can exercise that kind of power, how much more should a person whose spirit has been made alive by the Holy Spirit experience victory!

God knows your battles are in the Spirit, so He gave you spiritual weapons. He gave you access into the Spirit realm.

You have nothing to fear, so be strong and gird yourself. If you will fight, you will win!

Spiritual Warfare

It is not necessary to spend a lot of time addressing the devil. I am amazed at the lack of understanding in this area in the Body of Christ.

I am continually in churches and in Christian meetings across this country that begin in prayer. Yet, it never fails that eventually, attention is turned away from God to "rebuking" the devil.

Rebuking the devil isn't opening your mouth and saying, "I rebuke you." If you have invited the Holy Spirit into the service, the devil will go! We spend too much valuable time, which should be given to God, talking and singing to the devil.

Praise and worship are powerful weapons in spiritual warfare. I can't find Scripture to support the idea of singing to the devil. Yet, in some churches across the country, they are supposedly doing battle by singing to the devil and the spirits of darkness. Satan always wanted praise and worship directed to him. It doesn't matter whether it's good attention or bad attention. He just wants your attention.

Praise and worship are designed to lift up the Lord. If you lift Him up, He will take care of the devil, for when God arises, His enemies are scattered!

In 2 Chronicles 20, Jehoshaphat was instructed to have the singers and praisers lead the way into battle. Notice what they sang: "**. . . Praise the Lord, for his mercy endureth for ever**" (Verse 21). As they focused their attention on God, He took care of the enemy.

Satan is not the ruler of the world. He is the ruler of the *darkness of this world* (Ephesians 6:12). If you have been translated out of darkness and you are walking in the light, then what authority does Satan have? (1 Peter 2:9).

Therefore, true spiritual warfare is living in the Spirit and walking in the Word which allows Jesus' light to shine more perfectly through you. Wherever the light shines, darkness must flee and Satan's influence is diminished.

31
Spiritual Authority

Everyone needs someone! No matter how great the call or how grand the dream, you need others to help you reach your full potential.

God didn't create you to live in isolation. Church history is cluttered with the remains of people who had great plans, yet because they isolated themselves from others, they failed. Each of us need people around us whose input brings balance and stability to our lives.

A pastor who loves you, feeds you and encourages you when you are right and rebukes you when you are wrong is invaluable to your success.

Besides the relationship you have with your spouse and family, God will use your pastor to have the single greatest long-term effect in your life. That is a pretty strong statement. Yet, if people understood how important ministry is in their life, they would be more serious in choosing their pastor and in obeying the Holy Spirit in this area.

32
The Genesis Law

The Genesis Law is, "Everything reproduces after its own kind." Did you know someone's spirit is getting on you? When a person enters your life, they not only bring their body, experiences and opinions. They also bring their spirit.

Many successful people have learned the law of association, which is, "You will be like whoever you associate with."

Proverbs 13:20 says:

> He that walketh with wise men shall be wise: but a companion of fools shall be destroyed.

If you want to soar with eagles, you must quit running around with turkeys. In short, that is the law of association.

There is, however, another law which precedes the law of association. It is known as "the Genesis Law," which means "everything reproduces after its own kind."

> And God said, Let the earth bring forth grass, the herb yielding seed, and the fruit tree yielding fruit *after his kind*....
>   Genesis 1:11

In Genesis 1:21,24-25, God speaks of the Genesis Law of reproducing after its own kind:

> And God created great whales, and every living creature that moveth, which the waters brought forth abundantly, *after their kind,* and every winged fowl *after his kind:* And God saw that it was good.
>
> And God said, Let the earth bring forth the living creature *after his kind,* cattle, and creeping thing, and beast

of the earth *after his kind:* and it was so.

And God made the beast of the earth *after his kind*, and cattle *after their kind*, and every thing that creepeth upon the earth *after his kind*: and God saw that it was good.

This same law is true in the spiritual realm. *Everything produces after its own kind.* It is the Genesis Law, and you can't get away from it. That is why the person in authority over you is so important.

**Show me a pastor who is filled with unbelief,
and I'll show you people filled with unbelief.**

**Show me a pastor who runs down his people,
and I'll show you people who run down their pastor.**

**Show me a pastor of faith, power and vision,
and I'll show you people of faith, power and vision.**

The law of association is powerful, but the Genesis Law is stronger, because even if all of your associates are eagles, if those who birthed you were turkeys, then you are a turkey.

I can hear you screaming: "I was born a turkey, but can't I become an eagle?" The good news is, YES!

In the natural realm, once an animal is born, it has no choice of destiny. But in the realm of the Spirit, you can choose to change into a vessel of gold, silver, wood or earth (2 Timothy 2:20). You can be a sheep, goat or wolf, or in this case, a turkey or an eagle!

In the natural realm, there is no system of logic or choice by which an animal determines those who will affect his development. He moves by instinct, which has predetermined that "birds of a feather flock together."

In the Spirit realm, God made you a free moral agent. Therefore, you can, by a matter of choice, decide who is in authority over you. Many people are unsuccessful, because they are under the wrong pastor or under wrong leadership.

33
Submission to Authority

Submission comes from the person of lower position and authority. To have a proper relationship with your pastor, you need to be in submission to him. No one can impose submission upon you.

The man is ordained of God to be the head of his home. However, if the wife doesn't give him the right to be in authority, he is head over nothing! He cannot make her submit. The right to be in authority must be given.

Submission is not a female word. Men must learn to deal with their pride and ego and submit to one another in spiritual authority as God intended. I have noticed that many men who complain because their family won't recognize their authority are usually men who don't recognize their pastor's authority. If honor is to be received, it must first be given.

Submission to a pastor does not mean the pastor runs your life. He does not make your decisions for you. It doesn't mean he is better than you. If you are smart, you will recognize the need to have this godly person in your life to whom you must give the right to instruct, teach, correct and be a pastor to you.

Proverbs 12:15 says:

> **The way of a fool is right in his own eyes: but he that hearkeneth unto counsel is wise.**

Don't look for someone to take the place of the Holy Spirit in your life. Lay people, as well as pastors, allow themselves to be put into wrong positions. You don't need someone to tell you what car to buy, which house to purchase, who to marry or to discern all of your situations. Yet, many Christians are asking their pastor to make these decisions for them.

You can hear from God for yourself. The responsibility of your pastor is to feed you the Word of God so you can judge what you feel in your spirit by God's standard.

Find a real pastor by using the requirements for his position as set forth in the Word of God.

> **This is a true saying, If a man desire the office of a bishop, he desireth a good work.**
>
> **A bishop then must be blameless, the husband of one wife, vigilant, sober, of good behaviour, given to hospitality, apt to teach;**
>
> **Not given to wine, no striker, not greedy of filthy lucre; but patient, not a brawler, not covetous;**
>
> **One that ruleth well his own house, having his children in subjection with all gravity;**
>
> **(For if a man know not how to rule his own house, how shall he take care of the church of God?)**
>
> **Not a novice, lest being lifted up with pride he fall into the condemnation of the devil.**
>
> **Moreover he must have a good report of them which are without; lest he fall into reproach and the snare of the devil.**
> **1 Timothy 3:1-7**

There are many other passages of Scripture that give you information by which you should choose your pastor. Are you in agreement with what your pastor is hearing from God? Are there qualities and giftings God has given him that you want to affect your life? Is he a person of strength and character? Is he a person of integrity who faithfully represents God no matter what the consequences? Select him with Biblical wisdom, for he is reproducing *you* after his own kind.

When you find a godly pastor, stick with him. Never take your relationship for granted. Support him, pray for him, free him to be what God has called him to be.

There are few relationships this side of heaven greater than that of a pastor who is for his people, and people who are for their pastor — both for God and God for both.

34
Edifying Communication

The Body of Christ must learn to hear the right things and speak the right things. We learned the importance and power of a positive confession during the faith movement. We learned to speak, not what we had or what we felt, but what we wanted to have.

> ...Have faith in God.
>
> For verily I say unto you, That whosoever shall say unto this mountain, Be thou removed, and be thou cast into the sea; and shall not doubt in his heart, but shall believe that those things which he saith shall come to pass; he shall have whatsoever he saith.
>
> Mark 11:22-23

It is necessary that we learn to order our conversation by the guidelines of God's Word.

> ...and to him that ordereth his conversation aright will I shew the salvation of God.
>
> Psalm 50:23

To live at the level of success God has planned for you, you need to allow your heart and mind to become so full of His Word that it is natural for you to speak it out. I am a firm believer in the power of a positive confession. I believe in calling those things which are not as though they already exist. God created His world by words, and we can create our world by what we say, too.

BUT DON'T STOP THERE!

Many people master the principle of confession, yet they fail to allow the same Word to bring about a transformation in all areas of communication. Your words should not be filled with faith and excitement only when addressing God. On the contrary, they should minister love, grace and edification to all who hear.

> **Let no corrupt communication proceed out of your mouth, but that which is good to the use of edifying, that it may minister grace unto the hearers.**
> **Ephesians 4:29**

Learn to ask yourself when you are conversing with others:

*Is what I am saying good?
*Is it edifying?
*Is it ministering grace to those who are hearing it?

Too many times, we allow things to come out of our mouth that either short-circuit or cut the anointing of God out of our lives.

Let me tell you about a pastor for whom I preached years ago. As the Body of Christ increased, his ministry decreased. It concerned me, because God is not the author of lack. He is the author of abundance. This man's ministry kept decreasing to the point there was no anointing in the church.

I believe the problem in that particular ministry was they never learned to get a grip on their lip. Each time I went there, they were upset with someone new. One week it was a certain ministry they talked about, and the next week it was someone else. They felt because they weren't in agreement with someone, they were justified in slandering, speaking evil and gossiping about them.

Just because someone does you wrong doesn't give you the right to talk about them. This is an area of maturity we need to deal with and learn, as God's people, to put a guard on our lips.

There are people in the Body of Christ who will never be effective, because they feel like it's their right to critique and judge ministries and talk openly about them. They've lost the anointing off of their lives and don't even know it. They're like Samson. One day they will shake themselves and nothing will be there.

God never gave any person the right to feel justified in talking bad about people. Is it good? Is it edifying? Is it ministering grace to those who hear it?

Some people allow themselves to feed off of the spirit of gossip. They're not happy unless they've got something or someone to talk about. In this manner, they develop a dangerous appetite. It turns into a lifestyle. They become busybodies!

> **And withal they learn to be idle, wandering about from house to house; and not only idle, but tattlers also and busybodies, speaking things which they ought not.**
> **1 Timothy 5:13**

This speaks of talebearers. They go from one place to another as busybodies. The only business you are to be concerned about is *your* business.

If we don't watch ourselves, we will allow words to come out of our mouths that should never be said. If you have ever found yourself at the end of the day saying, "God, I should never have said that. Forgive me for what I said," then try this. When you wake up in the morning, say, "Father, *let no corrupt communication come out of my mouth.*"

Society has taught us that we need to express ourselves. They say, "Let your feelings out!" God says, "Control yourself and master your feelings or they will master you." Just because you have feelings doesn't mean you are supposed to let anyone else in on them. If some folks are having a bad day, everyone around them knows about it.

It amazes me the people who are recipients of gossip. In all the years that I've worked with other pastors and ministries, I never had the problem of people coming to me to gossip about someone else because they knew if they did,

I would rebuke them. I would tell them to be quiet and mind their own business in Jesus' name.

My ears aren't garbage cans. If you always know the latest gossip, you are just as bad as the person speaking it because you are listening to it. Guard not only what you say, but also what you hear and who you hear it from.

We've all heard people say, "Have you heard about So-and-so?" They wrap their gossip up in a spiritual garment! Or, "We need to pray for Brother So-and-so." Just because you are praying about someone doesn't give you the right to gossip about them.

Others think because they're being honest, they have the right to talk. There's a difference between honesty and truth. You can be honest and be wrong. Example: "You need to pray for Brother So-and-so. I honestly feel like he's against me." You might be wrong. Just because you are honest doesn't mean you should talk about it.

Don't let your feelings dictate what comes out of your mouth. Let the Word of God dictate what comes out of your mouth.

Let's assume you take someone under your wing to help nurture them, and they become your special project. Just because they are your "project" doesn't give you the privilege of dissecting their problems and distributing them to whomever you feel is worthy to know about them.

People have many times been hurt because they went to someone in confidence and that person betrayed the confidence by using personal information against them. It is sad when someone in the church has a problem, and the whole church knows about it before the next Sunday service. People who talk about others so badly in the church can be assured that unless they purify their own hearts, their relatives probably won't ever get saved!

35
Judging Every Conversation

There are three questions you can ask to judge every conversation:

1. Is it true?
2. Is it necessary?
3. Is it edifying?

Is it True?

If someone starts to tell you something about someone who is absent from the conversation, stop them and ask, "Is it true?" I'm not talking about asking them if it came from a reliable source. Just because it came from a reliable source doesn't mean it isn't gossip!

Is it Necessary?

Just because something is true doesn't mean you need to tell everyone about it. Is it necessary? People will say, "Did you know that Preacher So-and-so off in such-and-such a city quit the ministry and backslid?" Just because it's true doesn't mean you need to tell everyone about it.

Is it Edifying?

Does it minister grace, not only to the hearer, but to the one you are talking about? Ask yourself, "How is what I am saying going to affect the person I am talking about? How are others going to perceive this person after our conversation? Is it true? Is it necessary? Is it edifying?"

Proverbs 18:21 says, **"Death and life are in the power of the tongue...."** We need to learn to uphold and encourage one another. When I was growing up, I was always told, "If you can't say something good, don't say anything at all." Just because you have an opinion doesn't mean you need to express it. Just because you are being honest doesn't mean you need to share everything.

If you can't minister something that is edifying or say something that is full of grace, then you need to ask God to put a guard on your lips and let no corrupt communication come out of your mouth!

36
Energize Your Conversation With Positive Proverbs Power!

One day as I was reading in Proverbs, I realized that it had a lot to say about the words we speak. Proverbs many times describes the fool as someone who speaks too often and tells everything he knows or is known by his many words. On the other hand, the wise man is spoken of as the one whose words are measured, thought out, true and edifying.

I would encourage you to go through Proverbs and note the many references that link your success with God and man to communication. Let me help you to get started by sharing five short but powerful portions from Proverbs.

1. *Proverbs 10:20-21* — **The tongue of the just is as choice silver: the heart of the wicked is little worth.**

The lips of the righteous feed many: but fools die for want of wisdom.

2. *Proverbs 12:17-19* — **He that speaketh truth sheweth forth righteousness: but a false witness deceit.**

There is that speaketh like the piercings of a sword: but the tongue of the wise is health.

The lip of truth shall be established for ever: but a lying tongue is but for a moment.

3. *Proverbs 13:2-3* — **A man shall eat good by the fruit of his mouth: but the soul of the transgressors shall eat violence.**

He that keepeth his mouth keepeth his life: but he that openeth wide his lips shall have destruction.

4. *Proverbs 15:1-4* — A soft answer turneth away wrath: but grievous words stir up anger.

The tongue of the wise useth knowledge aright: but the mouth of fools poureth out foolishness.

The eyes of the Lord are in every place, beholding the evil and the good.

A wholesome tongue is a tree of life: but perverseness therein is a breach in the spirit.

5. *Proverbs 16:13* — Righteous lips are the delight of kings; and they love him that speaketh right.

Do you feel the power of God rising up in you as you speak these powerful and positive words? This is a powerful tool, not only to help you soar, but to help maintain your attitude once you are soaring.

37
The Destructiveness of Repeating Negatives

Noah is one of the great men of faith in the Old Testament. His ark stands forever as a symbol of man's unlimited ability to accomplish the impossible through faith.

After Noah's ark had safely housed his family and the remnant of animals, something drastic occurred. The Bible says that *Noah planted a vineyard and got drunk.*

> **And Noah began to be an husbandman, and he planted a vineyard:**
>
> **And he drank of the wine, and was drunken; and he was uncovered within his tent.**
> **Genesis 9:20-21**

God's man of faith and preacher of righteousness is lying in his tent drunk and naked.

Now, let's look at Verse 22:

> **And Ham, the father of Canaan, saw the nakedness of his father,** *and told his two brethren without.*

I believe his nakedness is a type of what we would call shortcomings, being undone or in a fallen state of sin. What should be done when you see someone's nakedness? Ham did as many of God's people do today. He told others the weakness and human frailty he had seen.

> **And Shem and Japheth took a garment, and laid it upon both their shoulders, and went backward,** *and covered the nakedness of their father....* (Verse 23).

Some Shall Soar!

When Noah awoke, he spoke a curse upon Canaan, which included Ham and his descendants, yet he blessed Shem and Japheth.

38
Our Tent of Covering

The tent was a place for family to fellowship and it was for safety and closeness. The tent is symbolic of covenant relationships.

Jesus is our tent of covering. As born-again believers, we are *in* Christ. God deals with our nakedness *inside* the tent of covering.

Ham took what he knew by virtue of close relationship and took it *outside* the tent to expose it. Great leaders of the Christian faith have reminded us through their nakedness that we are all human. Yet, God wants us, even in these situations, to keep a guard on our lips.

We don't need to run outside the tent and tell the media or every sinner in town what is wrong. We need to take a blanket of love and cover them, for love covers a multitude of sins. God will deal with the people in these situations, but God loves us so much He always deals with us in the tent of our covering, Jesus Christ.

Ham was cursed. What he spoke was true. It was factual, but it was not good, edifying, or full of grace.

Speak good, not evil. Seek to restore those who have sinned. Be an instrument of grace, not judgment. Keep yourself pure from gossip, and God will keep you under the tent of His covering.

39
Fitly Joined Together

> From whom the whole body fitly joined together and compacted by that which every joint supplieth, according to the effectual working in the measure of every part, maketh increase of the body unto the edifying of itself in love.
>
> Ephesians 4:16

The very nature of the Gospel and Christianity is based upon relationships. That's why the enemy comes in and tries to destroy God-ordained relationships. Unless you have a relationship with someone that is built in a godly manner, it is very hard to minister to that person or to receive ministry from them. The Gospel is people oriented, and people are relational.

There have been times the enemy has crept into good relationships and robbed people of the blessing of the relationship. Perhaps you have a friend who was dear and close, yet through misunderstanding or confusion, the person you valued so highly was stripped from your life.

I'm sure you have experienced tensions and struggles in your family when the devil worked overtime to try to pull you apart. He wants to ruin you, leaving you with a wounded spirit and bitter memories.

The enemy has schemes going on in the church, too. If he can't get the Word out of you, he will try to get you out of the Word, which means he will stop at nothing to separate you from the place which brings you the Word.

God's plan is for victory, even in relationships, for we are to be "**...joined and knit together by every joint with which it is supplied, when each part is working properly,**

makes bodily growth and upbuilds itself in love" (Ephesians 4:16, RSV).

The underlying thought is evident. We all have a part in the Body of Christ. If each person doesn't find his place, the Body's ability is diminished. Each person is important and of great value in God's perspective.

40
Individual and Corporate Mentality

There are many areas in relation to salvation in which each person stands alone. The decisions, actions, or perceptions of others have no bearing on our ability to grow in a desired direction. We enjoy this about Christianity. It is personal. You sink or swim on your own in a sense.

Yet, what seems to be painfully true is that there are also areas in which God views us corporately. We are sometimes lumped, knit and fitly joined together. We are individuals, yet not isolated.

When we speak of spiritual warfare, we are called an *army*. When we deal with beliefs and doctrines, we are referred to as *the household of faith*. When we submit to God's government, we are a *holy nation*. When we talk about fellowship and relationships, we become a *family*. When operating in praise and worship, we are a *temple*. When we speak of practical functioning, we are a *Body*.

It is impossible for you to be great in God's eyes if you are divorced from the rest of His Body.

Alone, you are not the army; you are a soldier.

Alone, you are not the Body; you are a member.

Alone, you are not the temple; you are a living stone.

Alone, you are not the nation; you are a citizen.

God sees you as an individual, yet He also deals with you in terms of those with whom you are in relationship.

Some Shall Soar!

AS AN ARMY, WE DEMONSTRATE.
AS A HOUSEHOLD OF FAITH, WE EDUCATE.
AS A HOLY NATION, WE RECIPROCATE.
AS A FAMILY, WE COHABITATE.
AS A TEMPLE, WE CONGREGATE.
AS A BODY, WE OPERATE.

Don't isolate yourself. No man is an island. When you walk in relationship to others, you are blessed and you are a blessing. You encourage while yet being encouraged. You use gifts to edify while being edified by the gifts of others.

Godly relationships bring maturity, responsibility and accountability.

41
Accountability

If you plan to achieve great things in God's name, you need the safety net of accountability. There should be people in your life that you have given the right to ask you hard questions, probing questions, soul-searching questions.

Obviously, it would be foolish to give that right to just anyone. Privates do not evaluate other privates. The general not only has the right, but he has the responsibility to bring his men into accountability. The same truth is evident in God's order for the home. Parents must bring their children into accountability for their actions.

As a pastor, I have the responsibility of bringing those under my oversight into accountability. It's not always fun, but it is necessary. There is no way out of it. I must ask hard questions. I must challenge people's priorities, confront sin, reprove, rebuke and instruct, all the while praying that I will help to save their souls from the snare of the devil.

I have had some people thank me for helping to guide them back in the right direction. I have had others challenge my right to do so and leave in an attitude of anger.

What can I say? Some will soar, while others will only be average — or less.

There are benefits to accountability. Let's look at a few of them.

1. *Accountability keeps you doctrinally in balance.*

It is vital that you receive a consistent diet of doctrinally-sound nourishment. It will build a solid foundation of truth in which you can anchor. Therefore, even in the midst of the emphasis of a particular truth in your life, you will never get out into the dangerous waters of extremism.

2. *Accountability keeps you emotionally in check.*

Every person at some time in their life has had "blind spots" in their temperament. We need people around us who know when we are operating out of weakness or strength, those who can identify the difference between our being led or driven.

I am reminded of an interview I watched with the great Gospel singer, Andre Crouch. He talked about being able to handle the great accolades of people because his father and mother kept him in check. Andre said his parents knew when he was really anointed or just performing. Everyone needs that type of godly relationship.

3. *Accountability keeps you built up spiritually.*

When you are involved in godly relationships, the Father always has an open avenue to encourage you through His great family. You are edified by others who are going through the same growth process as you are. Through prayer, worship, or just casual conversation, a rich deposit is made into your spirit. Many times, God speaks to us through one another if we will just stop and listen!

4. *Accountability keeps you going when you feel like quitting.*

To know that someone is "checking" on you can become a powerful motivational tool. You know what I mean. You wake up on Sunday morning and really don't want to get out of bed. Then you start thinking, "If I miss church, everyone will ask me where I was. If they find out I just took the day off, I will never hear the end of it."

Have you ever noticed the best services always occur when you miss? Everyone will tell you, "You should have been there. It was the best service we've ever had."

So even though you are tired and your flesh doesn't feel like getting up, you motivate yourself to rise up out

Accountability

of the bed, go to God's house and you are always glad you did.

That, my friend, is the power of accountability. It keeps you going when you feel like quitting!

42
Preserving Good Relationships

I want to share with you five guidelines for preserving good relationships.

1. *Alleviate unrealistic expectations.*

Don't expect from others that which you don't first expect from yourself.

A husband notices every extra pound on his wife's body while overlooking his own ever-increasing waistline.

A parishioner exclaims, "I want a pastor who is at His church every Sunday," yet misses regularly himself.

Get the picture? You can preserve relationships by freeing people from unrealistic expectations of them, and you will be happier if you learn not to try to live up to others' expectations of you.

Pastors aren't spiritual *all* the time.

Christian leaders' children go through developmental stages just like everyone else.

Great Gospel singers still hit flat notes.

Secretaries don't remember everything!

Just because someone has an office, a desk, or a position of prestige doesn't mean he is infallible.

All too often we see our own faults more clearly revealed in those who are closest to us. What we dislike about ourselves we really dislike in others. Every relationship needs tolerance and give and take — mostly give! So keep on giving and living.

2. *In today's relationships, don't respond out of yesterday's hurts.*

Relationships must stand on their own merit. Don't judge one another by someone else's character. It is easy to do, especially if you have been hurt deeply by someone for whom you cared. Then it becomes harder to trust, to love and forgive.

Let me give you an example. A man and woman are married. Everything seems to be going smoothly. She wishes he would communicate more, but doesn't worry much about it. After all, he has been working late a lot and someday they will have more time together. So she thought. Her whole world shattered when she found out her husband was seeing another woman. The result: divorce. The marriage ends, but the hurt still exists.

Five years later, this woman meets a man. They become engaged and then they marry. Shortly after their honeymoon, his boss expects him to work late to finish a project. When the husband tells his wife that he must work late, it brings negative feelings to the surface that have been buried for the last five years and which have never been dealt with.

Her natural reaction is to say to herself, "I've been through this before!" When he comes home, he gets the third degree. "I don't believe you were working," she says. "Why do you smell so nice?"

This pattern is repeated every time her husband does something that reminds her of her previous hurt. She is judging her husband by someone else's character. Instead of being the victim, she becomes the perpetrator, and he is the victim. He really was working late! He really does love her. Their relationship is being destroyed because one party is relating to the other out of a previous hurt.

If you are holding someone responsible for the actions of another, I pray the Holy Spirit will reveal it to you.

Liberate that person, and your relationship will be preserved.

3. *Don't play God.*

Some people are only in relationships where they are in control. They manipulate others by pouting or through anger. Others become emotional hostages.

Playing God means you get upset whenever someone doesn't do what *you* think they should do.

There are people in churches who are always upset. They see a new convert a few weeks old in the Lord exhibiting behavior from their previous lifestyle. Immediately, they are upset and no longer want anything to do with the baby Christian. They are playing God. The offended brother forgets that God spent many months working on him and will probably have to do the same with the new convert.

As God promotes you to new levels of authority, always be on guard for those who want to control you. It may come through money, prestige or an open door. Receive nothing that comes with strings attached.

Let God deal with others, and you won't be lording over them. Let God deal with you, and no one will be able to lord over you.

4. *Give no place to the devil by keeping the roles right!*

The word *place* means "area of influence." Give no area of influence to the devil. You need to keep all relationships *above board.*

If you're married, watch out for those who always want your time and attention, but never want your mate around. If you are single, don't spend hours alone with your boyfriend/girlfriend at each other's residences. You may ask, "Don't you trust us?" Yes, but I don't trust the devil! Never give him the opportunity to act upon a compromising situation.

As a pastor, I never counsel women in my office unless there are other staff members nearby. I trust myself. I have a wonderful wife. I trust most of those whom I counsel. But I don't trust the devil.

A person could get upset, run out of the office and swear I made an advance toward them when nothing happened. Then it would be my word against theirs. Therefore, I don't do very much personal counseling, and I do even less for women. I do none without someone else around.

If you value your relationships, shut all the devil's doors. Lock them tight. Keep him out.

5. *When your relationship with God is right, other relationships will be right.*

Much of the time, we get out of relationship with others when we get out of fellowship with God. When things aren't going well between you and God, you are unhappy with yourself, which makes you unhappy with others.

Our relationships work vertical first, then horizontal. If you keep your fellowship with God open (vertical), He will help you keep your personal dealings with others in proper order (horizontal).

Unforgiveness, bitterness, jealousy, envy and all of these emotions which are directed at others are the result of a broken relationship with God.

Build all personal relationships with Jesus in the middle. Keep Him as your best friend, and He will lead you into many wonderful relationships.

43
One Last Word!

God has called you to greatness. When all of this life's accomplishments are laid upon the altar of God and His holy fire puts them to the test, only what has been done in His name will remain. On that day when every person is rewarded according to his works, you will be glad you chose to break out of the ranks of "average."

I leave you with the word of this poem, which I pray will keep you flying high with Jesus!

The path I chose to walk
    To others seemed long and hard,
For I chose to value godly things
    That others chose to discard.
While dreaming dreams of heavenly things,
    My heart grew in grace and strength.
Therefore, I did not notice my load,
    My trouble nor the journey's length.
For along the way, great peace I found,
    As my will gave way to His commands.
Thus, safely the Lord He led me on,
    Through new, uncharted lands.
One day my journey did come to a close,
    And I from my labor did rest.
With head held high, "Dear Lord," said I,
    "You know I gave my best!"